LET'S GO HUNTING

Hunting MOOSE and ELK

Hines Lambert

PowerKiDS press
New York

Published in 2013 by The Rosen Publishing Group, Inc.
29 East 21st Street, New York, NY 10010

First Edition

Editor: Amelie von Zumbusch
Book Design: Kate Laczynski

Photo Credits: Background graphic © iStockphoto.com/Andrea Zanchi; sidebar binoculars © iStockphoto.com/Feng Yu; cover Stephen Krasemann/All Canada Photos/Getty Images; p. 5 Steve Bower/Shutterstock.com; p. 6 William Albert Allard/National Geographic/Getty Images; pp. 7, 24 iStockphoto/Thinkstock; p. 9 Steven Kaufman/Peter Arnold/Getty Images; p. 10 James Hager/Robert Harding World Imagery/Getty Images; p. 11 Volodymyr Burdiak/Shutterstock.com; p. 12 Gregory Johnston/Shutterstock.com; p. 13 Robert Kelsey/Shutterstock.com; p. 14 Nate A./Shutterstock.com; p. 15 Warren Price Photography/Shutterstock.com; p. 16 eans/Shutterstock.com; p. 17 7505811966/Shutterstock.com; pp. 19, 20 Justin Kral/Shutterstock.com; p. 21 RubberBall Productions/the Agency Collection/Getty Images; p. 23 Mike Kemp Images/The Image Bank/Getty Images; p. 25 Jonathan Nackstrand/AFP/Getty Images; p. 26 Jack Dagley Photography/Shutterstock.com; p. 27 (left) Joshua Caldwell/Flickr/Getty Images; p. 27 (right) Hans Berggren/Johner Images/Getty Images; p. 28 Philippe Henry/Oxford Scientific/Getty Images; p. 29 George D. Leep/Photo Researchers/Getty Images.

Library of Congress Cataloging-in-Publication Data

Lambert, Hines.
Hunting moose and elk / by Hines Lambert. — 1st ed.
p. cm. — (Let's go hunting)
Includes index.
ISBN 978-1-4488-9663-9 (library binding) — ISBN 978-1-4488-9784-1 (pbk.) —
ISBN 978-1-4488-9785-8 (6-pack)
1. Moose hunting—Juvenile literature. 2. Elk hunting—Juvenile literature. I. Title.
SK302.L36 2013
799.2'7657—dc23

2012027386

Manufactured in the United States of America

CPSIA Compliance Information: Batch #W13PK2: For Further Information contact Rosen Publishing, New York, New York at 1-800-237-9932

CONTENTS

Big Game

Big game like moose and elk present some of the most challenging hunting in North America. They often live in **wildernesses** or **nature preserves**. This can make them difficult to find. They live in only a handful of the 50 states. Hunting trips for moose and elk are often like vacations. Hunters must take days off from school and work.

Elk and moose are members of the deer family, but they are far bigger than deer. Their size makes them harder to kill than most other game. Elk and moose hunters enjoy the challenge. Big-game hunting is becoming more popular every year.

Moose and elk hunters work hard to kill animals, but they also work hard to save animals. Big-game hunters donate more money to **conservation** than any other type of hunter.

Did You Know?

The meat from elk and moose is delicious and nutritious. It is lower in fat and cholesterol than most beef.

North Americans use the name moose for this animal. Confusingly, animals of the same species that live in Europe and Asia are called Eurasian elk.

Know the Law

Each state has different hunting rules. You should check the website of your state's wildlife office. It will tell you when you can hunt, where you may go, and the **bag limit** for each animal.

Since elk and moose are not found in every state, you may have to travel to another state to hunt them. Licenses for out-of-state hunters can be expensive!

Hunting laws are in place to make sure that populations of big game and other hunted animals stay healthy.

Most states issue tags for each moose or elk a hunter Is allowed to kill. There are different tags for hunting males, females, and calves.

The bag limits for these animals are usually pretty low. For example, Maine allows a hunter to kill only one moose each year, while Minnesota allows only one antlered moose for each group of two to four hunters. You may also find that the hunting season is short. Many states count the elk **population** each year in order to see how many licenses they may give out.

2,000 Burgers

Moose are the largest members of the deer family. A male moose, or bull, can weigh as much as 1,600 pounds (726 kg)! Its antlers alone can weigh 40 pounds (18 kg). A big bull will provide about 500 pounds (227 kg) of meat. That is enough for 2,000 quarter-pound (113 g) burgers!

Bulls grow antlers every summer, starting when they are about 6 or 7 years old. They fight with their antlers over which one will mate with females. Moose that are 10 to 12 years old have the biggest antlers. Most hunters want to shoot a moose that is this age.

The more you know about moose, the easier they are to find. Moose love eating willow leaves and birch shrubs. They are often found near rivers.

Did You Know?

Moose battles can be tough! In 2010, a hunter in Minnesota found the remains of two giant moose that had gotten their antlers stuck together and died fighting each other.

Most big-game hunters respect animals, enjoy being outdoors, and love nature.

Hard to Find

They might be big, but moose can be hard to find! Some hunters use calls to bring moose closer to them. Some calls are horns that sound like female moose, or cows. This is a great way to trick a big bull during mating season. Practice your call so that it sounds real, or a moose will not be fooled. Some hunters also buy scents that smell like cows. These are almost like perfume for moose!

Moose make many noises. Bull moose, like this one, grunt to challenge each other during the mating season.

In the summer months, moose tend to stay within a 2-mile (3 km) range of their homes, so your hunt may go better if you stay in one place.

When hunting moose, it is important to keep in mind that moose like things cool. They often go to higher ground and look for shade. They also like places that have recently been damaged by fires and logging, or the cutting down of trees. They like the plants that grow in these places.

Elk Are Tough

Can you spot the bull that joined this elk herd?

Elk are much bigger than deer but smaller than moose. Four **subspecies** of elk are found in North America. Male elk, called bulls, can weigh up to 700 pounds (318 kg). Female elk, called cows, live with their young in herds. Bulls live alone until mating season. During mating season, a bull will protect and mate with a group of cows. Other bulls will challenge him.

Sometimes male elk fight to the death over cows. Their antlers make good weapons.

Did You Know?

Elk may look slow, but they can actually run at speeds of up to 40 miles per hour (64 km/h).

Elk **migrate** with the seasons. There are about one million elk in the United States. They live in many different **habitats**, from desert to thick forest. Most elk live in western states, such as Colorado, Arizona, and New Mexico.

Elk are also called wapiti. This is a Native American name that comes from the Shawnee and Cree languages.

Bugling

During winter, elk tend to be found on large, sunny slopes or eating in fields. They often bed down in forests on cold evenings to get protection from storms and frost. In warm weather, elk go into forests for shade. They can also be found standing in lakes or streams. Good elk hunters know how to track these animals. Elk tracks look like deer tracks but are larger.

This hunter is using an elk call. Practice your call at home before you use it on a hunt.

Some hunters make the mistake of bugling too much. This can make an elk angry, and angry bulls are known to charge!

Like moose, elk can be attracted by calls. Sporting stores sell several kinds of calls. Some look like whistles. Other calls are long horns. These long horns make a noise called **bugling**. If a bugling call is used correctly, a bull elk will answer back. This is a great way to locate a bull.

Did You Know?

Elk need to eat about 10 to 15 pounds (4.5–7 kg) of plants each day! Elk find watering holes but also get water from dew and juicy plants.

Bigger Calibers

The **rifle** is the most popular weapon for elk and moose hunting because it has such a long range. Because elk and moose are so large, they can be spotted from very far away. Good shots can hit big game from 400 yards (366 m) away.

If you are not sure which rifle to use, talk to an experienced big-game hunter.

It is important to choose a rifle with a good **caliber** for big game. Caliber is simply a measure of the width of the barrel of your rifle. A .30- or .30-6-caliber rifle is great for hunting elk or moose. These rifles use larger bullets than other hunting rifles. Big-game hunters usually use rifles that are higher caliber than many deer rifles.

Remember that big-game hunting is often like hiking. You must be in good shape to walk long distances while carrying your rifle.

A pair of binoculars can help you spot an elk or moose from far away. Then you can carefully move within range.

Aim Is Everything

Most moose and elk hunters use rifles with scopes. A scope is a small telescope that sits on your rifle. Your scope can help you see your target better. You will be able to make sure that it has antlers.

It is important to sight in your rifle. Ask an adult hunter to help you use a bore-sighting tool. The idea is to make sure your scope and your rifle are aiming at the same point so that your aim is true.

With elk and moose, the best shot is usually behind the tip of the shoulder. This way your shot will hit the heart or lungs and kill the animal quickly. A wounded elk can run very far, and you may never see it again.

This hunter is peering through his scope while on a big-game hunting trip in Wyoming.

Rifles Are Not Toys

Remember that your rifle is a dangerous weapon. If it can kill an animal that weighs more than 1,000 pounds (454 kg), imagine what it can do to you or another hunter.

The long range of a rifle also makes it dangerous, too. Always be aware of your surroundings. What will happen if your shot misses its target?

Never forget that you are carrying a dangerous weapon. Accidents happen when people are careless.

Many big-game hunters wear bright orange. This color is easy for other hunters to spot but hard for members of the deer family to see.

The bullet has to end up somewhere. Never shoot in the direction of homes, roads, or other hunters.

Keep your rifle's **safety** on until you are ready to fire. Never point your rifle at anything you do not wish to shoot. Try to be ready to shoot at all times, though. Many hunters tell stories about putting their rifles down for a few seconds only to have an elk or moose walk right by.

Poundage

Big-game hunting is difficult enough, but some hunters prefer an even greater challenge. They hunt moose and elk with bows. These animals are powerful, so they require bows that are also powerful. Bow power is measured in poundage. Moose and elk require at least 45 pounds, and most hunters choose even higher poundage.

Bow hunters must get much closer to their game before they shoot than rifle hunters do. Rifles can kill these animals from 400 yards (366 m) away, but bow hunters should be no farther than 100 yards (91 m) away. It is important to shoot the animal from a side angle. Moose and elk have too much muscle, fat, and bone for straight-on shots to work.

Since they need to get closer to shoot, big-game hunters who use bows need to be good at creeping up on elk and moose.

Big Dogs

Few hunters in the United States choose to hunt big game with dogs, but the right dog can make a difference. Swedish and Norwegian elkhounds are great for this sport. These breeds are ancient. Norwegian elkhounds are believed to have been around for at least 6,000 years. Karelian bear dogs, which originated in Finland, also make excellent big-game hunters.

Norwegian elkhounds are pack animals. They love families and are very loyal.

These dogs are bred to hunt large game like elk, moose, and even bears.

Hunting dogs can be trained to bark when they spot game. They can even chase the animals toward hunters. These dogs are athletic. They have lots of fur to keep them warm because, like the elk and moose they are used to hunt, they often live in cold areas.

Did You Know?

Herbert Hoover, who was president of the United States from 1929 until 1933, had a Norwegian elkhound named Weegie.

Big-game hunting with dogs is fairly common In Scandinavia. This hunter and his dog came from Norway to big-game hunt in Sweden.

Heavy Kills

Some hunters say that killing big game is the easy part. Remember, these are big animals! They can be very hard to move, especially if they die in brush. Unless your shot killed it instantly, you might have to locate your kill. Wounded moose, and especially elk, can travel quite a long way before they die.

It is key to **field dress** the animal correctly. Elk and moose meat taste delicious, but only if they are properly

This is an elk burger. Elk and moose meat tend to be milder tasting than deer meat.

Above: ***Hunters often hang big-game antlers on their walls. A person called a taxidermist can prepare the animal's entire head to be hung on the wall.*** **Right:** ***These hunters are getting ready to field dress the moose they shot.***

cut from the animals. It is important to bring a sharp knife and rope. Many big-game hunters bring bone saws and hatchets to help them cut up these tough animals. Bring a metal-frame backpack to help you carry the meat. Wrapping the meat in a material called cheesecloth helps keep it from spoiling.

Saving Big Game

Like many animals, moose and elk need to be protected. At one time, both species had low populations because hunters killed so many of them. Farmers used to shoot elk so that they could not steal food from their cattle. In recent years, hunters, environmental groups, and the government have been working together to make sure this never happens again.

Elk and moose hunters hunt in some of the wildest, most spectacular places in North America.

Moose are making a comeback. They are now being spotted in parts of the Northeast where they had once died out.

You can do your part, too. Be sure to use your kill. If all hunters use the meat from their kills and respect bag limits, the deaths of these animals are not wasteful. Remember that hunting laws are there to protect the animals. Bag limits keep moose and elk populations at healthy levels so that the animals will be around to challenge hunters for years to come.

HUNTING TIPS

1. Big-game hunting is an athletic sport. Get in shape! In addition to practicing with your weapon, practice hiking and running.

2. Elk can smell very well. Try to get downwind from them. This means the wind should blow from the elk to you.

3. After you have located your kill, wait 30 minutes before touching it to make sure it is dead. Elk and moose kicks can be powerful and dangerous.

4. Avoid spooking moose and elk. If the animals get scared and run, it will be hard to find them and attract them.

5. Consider using a bicycle, cart, or even a sled to help you carry out your meat.

6. If you want to stalk your prey, try to go right after it has rained. Because the ground is wet, your footsteps will be quiet.

7. Elk love barley and alfalfa. If you find a farmer, he may be happy to have you hunt nearby so that his crops are safe.

8. If you are new to an area, go out before your hunt to scout where the animals are. This way, you can move carefully and slowly on your hunting day.

GLOSSARY

bag limit (BAG LIH-mut) How many of a certain kind of animal a hunter is allowed to kill.

big game (BIG GAYM) Large wild animals that are hunted for food or sport.

bugling (BYOO-gul-ing) Making the kind of call bull elk do when mating.

caliber (KA-luh-ber) Having to do with how wide a gun's opening is.

conservation (kon-sur-VAY-shun) Protecting something from harm.

field dress (FEELD DRES) To remove the parts from a kill that would make the meat go bad.

habitats (HA-buh-tats) The kinds of land where animals or plants naturally live.

migrate (MY-grayt) To move from one place to another.

nature preserves (NAY-chur prih-ZERV-ez) Land set aside for animals and plants.

population (pop-yoo-LAY-shun) A group of animals or people living in the same area.

rifle (RY-ful) A long gun that is fired from the shoulder.

safety (SAYF-tee) A part on a gun that keeps it from being fired by mistake.

subspecies (SUB-spee-sheez) Different kinds of the same animal.

wildernesses (WIL-dur-nis-ez) Areas that have no lasting settlements.

INDEX

WEBSITES

Due to the changing nature of Internet links, PowerKids Press has developed an online list of websites related to the subject of this book. This site is updated regularly. Please use this link to access the list:
www.powerkidslinks.com/lgh/moose/